CITY LIFE

text by JEANNELLE FERREIRA
illustrations by J. CECELIA HAYTKO

graphic design NICOLE D'ISA and XAVAIRE BOLTON

CITY LIFE

ISBN 978 1 6070 1299 3

Printed in U.S.A.

I love to hear the train go by when streetlights brighten up the sky.

When my moms tuck me into bed, I think about the day ahead.

Tomorrow we will ride our bikes

to get the vegetables
we like.

At the museum

or the zoo

there will be lots of things to do.

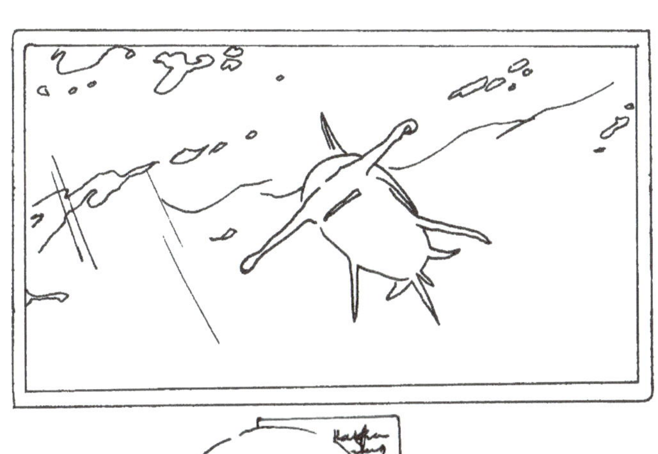

Maybe we can ride the bus

to see the hippopotamus!

We could get pretzels from a cart

(my moms give me the bigger part).

One last stop before it's dark

to feed the pigeons in the park.

At home again,
it's time to rest

I like city life the best.

Jeannelle Ferreira is the author of one book, two short stories, and three poems for adults. She lives in Maryland with her wife, their daughter, and many animals.

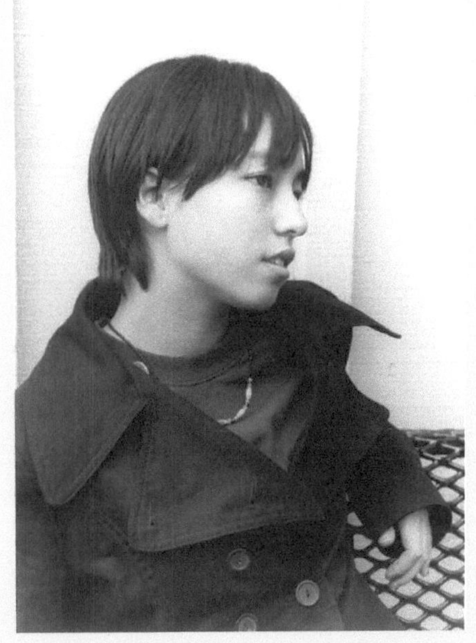

J. Cecelia Haytko is a traveling student and artist. If she had to live on one food for the rest of her life it would be clementines.

www.ingramcontent.com/pod-product-compliance
Ingram Content Group UK Ltd.
Pitfield, Milton Keynes, MK11 3LW, UK
UKHW060113300726
14090UKWH00002B/164

* 9 7 8 1 6 0 7 0 1 2 9 9 3 *